Ideas Plus

A Collection of Practical Teaching Ideas
Book One

National Council of Teachers of English
1111 Kenyon Road, Urbana, Illinois 61801

Staff Editor: Audrey Hodgins

Book Design: Tom Kovacs for TGK Design

NCTE Stock Number 22477

Library of Congress Catalog Card Number 84-3479

Contents

Foreword

This book was developed as part of the NCTE Plus membership. We hope you will find it a valuable resource, one that will help you to enliven your classroom and engage your students. We trust that it will also encourage you to reflect on your teaching, an important part of continued professional growth.

IDEAS Plus and its quarterly companion *NOTES Plus*, both new publications, are the principal benefits of NCTE Plus membership. The initial response to this new membership category and to these new publications has been overwhelming, in terms of subscriptions but especially in terms of ideas contributed. In fact, part of the very first volume of *IDEAS Plus* comes from contributions sent us by NCTE Plus members.

Although this book was assembled at headquarters, it was written by classroom teachers across the country. Thus *IDEAS Plus,* like *NOTES Plus,* enables teachers to share their best teaching practices and activities with each other. In publishing this collection, we hope to broaden the professional exchange that has always occurred among teachers—in workrooms, in department offices, and in classrooms after school.

In bringing together a collection of teaching activities like this one, we do not mean to suggest that the ideas should be used in isolation. Our intention is that you integrate these activities and ideas into existing curricula, units, and lessons, incorporating them in ways that reflect your own individual teaching style.

This first volume of *IDEAS Plus* is at the heart of the Council's mission—exchanging ideas and information in ways that improve the quality of our teaching.

1 Literature: They Can Take It with Them

It was Ezra Pound who remarked that literature is news that stays news, and so each year's crop of seniors experiences for itself and as if for the first time ever the psychological complexities of Shakespeare's plays and the bite of Swift's observations while their younger classmates participate in the secret life of the surprising Mr. Mitty and discover what it means to float down the Mississippi on a raft. The activities that follow suggest ways of extending the study of literature through oral interpretation, through historical investigation, through the visual arts, and of course through the complex psychological processes of empathy and identification. Several activities deal with specific works but most illustrate more general strategies that can be applied to a number of works.

Spoken Collage

I recommend this activity for getting students to take a closer look at poetry. It emphasizes the idea of theme in poetry, but it also provides an opportunity for students to polish their oral reading skills. It's an excellent way to end a poetry unit, but it's successful as an independent activity in creative dramatics.

Bring to class as many poetry texts and collections as possible. Song lyrics (Beatle lyrics are good) may be included. I also ask students to bring in poems and lyrics they have at home. Divide the class into groups of three or four and share the poetry materials. Students look through the collections and select three or four poems that they feel belong together in some significant way. They then recombine the poems to create a new impression (theme) or to reinforce the existing one. They may use poems in their entirety or select portions of them.

After students have assembled this verse collage, they must think of a way to present it to the class. Encourage them to experiment with the reading of their collage by using various members of their group in various ways. Changes in tempo and volume, the use of male or female voices, and choral and solo sections all affect the overall impression their production will leave with an audience. They may use background music or music to introduce or close the presentation.

1

Money, love, war, suicide, and school are among the themes my students have chosen, but the possibilities are many. One group chose the theme of loneliness and presented its collage in a darkened room. Members of the group wore black and sat in the four corners of the room, each illuminated only by a candle. As each reader finished, he or she blew out the candle. A group presenting a collage on old age produced a moving effect by backdropping their readers with a slide of an old man alone on a park bench. A collage on the rebelliousness of youth was presented by a group costumed as stereotyped hoods against the backdrop of a graffiti-covered wall.

Paula Lee, Queen Elizabeth School, Edmonton, Alberta

Ms. Boothby Sent Me

Transform your classroom into a speakeasy of the Roaring Twenties after your class has studied the literature of this remarkable decade, including in my classes Fitzgerald's *Great Gatsby* and Dreiser's *American Tragedy*. These five steps provide everything you need except the bathtub.

1. Through collaborative teaching students learn about the texture of American life during the Twenties. A music teacher lectures on the music of the Twenties, with recorded examples to listen to. An art teacher talks about the art of the decade; there's much to see here. A history teacher covers the major social changes that occurred during this period.

2. Each student is responsible for investigating a literary or other historical figure of the Twenties. Later, the student will assume the identity of this figure and visit our speakeasy.

3. The classroom is transformed into a speakeasy. Cover a wall, the chalkboard, a bulletin board, with the slang of the 1920s. Use an opaque projector to make a life-size flapper and escort. Decorate with pictures, postcards, photos, posters. Group the desks and cover them with checked paper tablecloths. Play period records (on an old cylinder phonograph if possible). Issue membership cards and devise a password.

4. On the day of the speakeasy, students dress in appropriate costume, present their membership cards, and state the password. During the class period each assumes the role of the researched character and converses on topics of the day from the point of view of that character—prohibition, fashion, fads, current events of the day. Interested faculty may attend—if they come in character and costume.

5. Finally, notify the staff of school publications and the local press for coverage.

Elaine S. Boothby, South River High School, Edgewater, Maryland

The Name Is Familiar, But I Can't Place the Face

As an ongoing assignment in a short story unit, I ask students to watch newspapers and magazines for "portraits" of characters from the stories we read. At the end of the unit, we set aside a day for mounting these pictures, identifying each with a label on the back. Then we share the pictures in class, attempting to identify the entire set. If necessary, we give clues—a favorite expression of the character, an object associated with that character, a brief quote from the story. Students enjoy the photo hunt and seem able to envision characters more sharply as they read.

Ed Van Vickle, Indian Valley North School, Midvale, Ohio

It's All in Your Point of View

Students (indeed, readers in general) tend to see action and dialogue between characters as the really important part of a novel or story. What many young readers fail to realize is that the narrator is often the most important character in the story: he or she *is* the storyteller, and we readers get whatever version of events the narrator chooses to tell. How he or she describes those events has a crucial impact on how we in turn interpret the story. The following exercise helps students appreciate the importance of narrative point of view as it gives them the opportunity to practice writing, oral reading, and acting skills.

As a homework assignment, ask each student to write two versions of a confrontation between two or more people—an incident they witnessed or participated in or an imaginary one. The important criteria are that the interaction center around some kind of conflict and that it take place between two or more characters. Two or three paragraphs suffice, though many students end up writing several pages.

If, for instance, I write about an argument between Mary and Tom, I might first describe the conflict from Mary's point of view and then from Tom's. But I also might choose to write from the point of view of another major participant in the action, or a person who knows the major participants but is only peripherally involved, or a third-person narrator who knows the thoughts of one or more of the characters, or an "objective" observer who merely reports what he or she sees and hears. The storyteller might even be an inanimate object; one student, for example, described two children fighting over a toy from the viewpoint of one of the youngsters and then through the eyes of the toy, peering out anxiously at the fight from where it had been kicked under the bed.

In class, read aloud both versions of these incidents and discuss differences created by point of view. Does the listener feel more or less sympathy for a given character in one version as opposed to the other? Do events seem to change when they are told through different eyes? Do you trust one storyteller more than the other?

Choose several scenes and ask class members to stage and perform both versions on the following day, demonstrating how drastically characterization, tone, and even events are altered by a change in narrative point of view. One girl, for example, had written about a monopoly game with her boyfriend. Performed from the viewpoint of a third-person narrator who was a sympathetic confidante of the boy, the game became an epic "battle of the sexes," with the girl humiliated by her defeat at the hands of a manly opponent. Viewing the scene through the girl's eyes, however, we saw not only that she was unruffled at losing the game but that she was amused by how seriously her boyfriend took a trivial game of chance.

Extend the activity to short stories and novels read by the class. I've had good success with Faulkner's "A Rose for Emily," asking students to write from the point of view of various characters in the story and to discuss how our perception of the story changes with the teller's point of view.

Paula Gray, Parkland Community College, Champaign, Illinois

Chrono-logs

Any novel lends itself to this activity but especially appropriate are those without chapter titles.

After students have read the first chapter of the assigned novel, ask them to prepare two statements that cover the most important events in that chapter. Students then convert their two statements into sentences to be completed and recopy them on a separate piece of paper. Suppose the assigned novel is *Where the Red Fern Grows*. A student might write the following initial statement: "In the opening scene Billy comes upon a violent dogfight." The incomplete or elliptical statement might read like this: "In the opening scene Billy comes upon a . . ."

Students then exchange elliptical statements with classmates, who complete the statements on separate sheets of paper. This simple device allows readers to check on their comprehension of main events in the plot. The sentence-completion exercise also serves as a review of what has been read so far. As successive chapters are assigned, students keep the completed sentences as a chrono-log that eventually becomes an outline of the novel's plot.

Jean K. Hammond, Northampton Middle School, Machipongo, Virginia

Think Theme

The idea of theme can be a difficult one for junior high students to grasp. I've found a way to sneak up on this somewhat nebulous notion.

I begin by asking volunteers to tell a favorite story or joke. After each story, I ask several other students to state the basic idea of the story or joke. From these thumbnail statements we work toward a definition of theme.

Then I ask each student in turn to name a favorite television show and to try to state its theme in one sentence. We refine our definition of theme based on this information.

Next we turn to "Black Boy" by Richard Wright, but other stories with lots of action will also serve. Students read excerpts and we discuss the story, working toward a statement of its theme. I divide the class into groups, and each group selects a scene from the story that illustrates the theme. Now the task is to plan a way to present this scene to the class. After adequate time for preparation, the dramatizations are given. Following each presentation, the class comments on how that scene and its dramatization reflect or develop the theme of "Black Boy."

Patricia H. Ford, Carol City Junior High School, Miami, Florida

Roses and Rage: Evaluating Short Stories

Into every unit of short story study comes the moment when we ask students to evaluate what they have read. When this moment comes, I introduce the Roses to the Author Awards and the I'd Like to Rip It Out of the Book Awards. For each of these, I ask students to come up with individual awards that reflect traditional categories of discussion. For example, roses may be presented for

Best Title

Most Interesting (Complex, Amusing) Character

The Theme I Most Wanted to Tell an Extraterrestrial About

The Story with Surprising Vocabulary

Reader's Choice

Having dealt with the positive side, we turn to pet peeves. Typical of the areas in which students elect to present awards are

The Empty-headed Theme

The I Wouldn't Send a Postcard from This Setting Award

The Squashed (least well-rounded) Character

Reader's Reject

When students have made their nominations, they write a paragraph in defense of one of their choices. These papers are shared, and I've generally found that they reflect, albeit in humorous fashion, fairly astute critical perceptions. Discussion is lively and devising awards and deciding on candidates are fun.

Larry Morehead, Cascade Middle School, Longview, Washington

Macbeth behind the Desk

I've had fun using John Updike's story "Tomorrow and Tomorrow and So Forth" after the class has read *Macbeth*. The story illustrates sustained literary allusion, but since it is set in a high school English class, it does much more. It's also a wonderful opportunity to work with Macbeth's soliloquy and to apply a bit of Aristotle's *Poetics* in a discussion of the tragic hero.

I begin by asking students to be responsible for these words from Updike's story: *infallible, barometric, annalistic, frieze, arrogance, generate, virtual, preposterous, premonition, oppressive, diffident, soliloquy, chivalrous, intercession, taut, beseechingly, rendition, coddling.* In return, I provide some information about Updike, including photographs.

Our discussion of the story focuses briefly on Updike's use of names: Brute Young is a "young brute," Gloria Angstrom is Mark's "glorious angst," Barry Snyder is "very snide," Peter *Forrest*er has a connection with Birnam *Wood*. We also explore Updike's use of weather to enhance the story's theme. In the first paragraph Mark guesses it will rain because of the "infallible barometric" reaction of his students. After Mark senses Geoffrey's premonition, he looks through the window: "The clouds were gaining in intensity." Then Prosser talks about the oppressive atmosphere and darkness in *Macbeth*. Later Teresa, Mark, and Gloria discuss the "cloud shadows" of the "tomorrow" soliloquy and Prosser notices that "beyond the windows actual clouds were bunching rapidly." After the buzzer sounds the end of the day, Mark notices that "the rain was coming down fast now," and in the final paragraph Mr. Prosser sees himself for what he is and pinches his fingers painfully as he puts his rubbers over his shoes.

We also touch on elements of Updike's style. His use of alliteration ("such sunny sentiments," "terrible truth," "said sideways softly"); his skill with simile ("minds like moths," "her short, brushed-up hair like a cool torch"—with the torch a pun on Prosser's feelings for Gloria and a suggestion of danger); and finally Updike's use of allusion. Macbeth's famous soliloquy about the meaninglessness of life enriches this story about a modern-day Macbeth. Mark is Updike's tragic antihero. He is not, as Aristotle writes, "better than ourselves"; he is "ourselves." Like Macbeth, his tragic flaw is pride. He manipulates his class to enhance his own superiority and from this "great height" falls as a tragic hero must. Macbeth is undone when Birnam Wood comes to Dunsinane; Mark is brought down by Peter Forrester, and like Macbeth, the sequence of events was provoked by a woman.

Sharon Thomas, Timberline High School, Lacey, Washington

When the World's the Stage

In my introduction to literature courses, students studying drama for the first time ask questions like these: "Why isn't there more action in *Oedipus Rex*?" "Why does *Hamlet* close with the bodies being carried off the stage?" I began to see that they were applying their knowledge of today's television and stage techniques (with their elaborate settings, freeze frames, close-ups, and the like) to these plays. I wanted them to continue doing this, but I also wanted them to understand the relationship between drama and its stage.

Models of a Greek theater or Shakespeare's Globe help to explain dramatic conventions. But to underscore that the answers to their questions involved, at least in part, the nature of the stage for which the plays were written, we recreated some of the stage conditions of Greek and Shakespearian drama.

We began by using as our stage the niche in the cafeteria set aside for faculty-staff dining. We read the last lines of the duel scene in *Hamlet*, positioned the bodies and stopped. Both actors and audience immediately recognized the awkwardness of having no curtain or house lights that could be lowered to cover the exits of the "dead" actors—and students began to understand one reason why the play ends as it does.

From the cafeteria we moved out in the sunlight to do a few lines from the balcony scene in *Romeo and Juliet*. Our sunny surroundings made the point that Shakespeare had to rely on language to create setting; today we would merely lower the stage lights.

We moved our troupe yet a third time. Students positioned on a bank overlooking the parking lot learned that an audience was not always able to see facial expressions and action taking place some distance away; and they could see why in a Greek play much of the action was created through dialogue.

Back in the classroom, we discussed what we had observed and how these scenes might be staged in today's theater or for television. Students, I think, developed a greater sense of a play as a staged performance, and we had fun considering these aspects of staging. The idea might be expanded to include other aspects of staging, for example, times when the audience is treated as a character in a play, which seems to happen in *Julius Caesar* when Antony reads Caesar's will.

Sara M. Miller, Northern Virginia Community College, Woodbridge, Virginia

Walking through *A Midsummer Night's Dream*

Recently a ninth-grade class had an opportunity to see *A Midsummer Night's Dream* performed by a college group. With no time to read the play, the teacher was concerned about how students would follow the many characters in the four interwoven plots. The simple procedure outlined below acquainted them with the main characters and helped them anticipate the unfolding of the plot.

On large squares of tagboard write the names of major characters, using coded colors for pairs and groups: blue for Theseus and Hippolyta, red for Oberon and Titania, and so on. Stack the cards in the order that the characters will be introduced.

As you tell the story, distribute each name card on cue and ask the recipient to assume the position referred to. Hermia and Helena and Lysander and Demetrius, for instance, should stay together—or move about—as you relate their actions. Students are both actors and audience and should study one another and try to remember names. (Students hold their name cards up squarely during the exercise so classmates can try to fix the names.) If you have more students than characters, ask some individuals to represent important objects in the play; give a purple flower to Charlie and let him be "Love in Idleness." Encourage at least minimal characterization: let Nick Bottom scratch his hairy face; suggest that Cobweb and Moth fan the queen as she reclines under an imaginary snake skin.

This playful introduction to *A Midsummer Night's Dream* helped students over the initial hurdle of sorting out the characters and plot. Certainly it enabled them to view the performance with greater insight and pleasure than would otherwise have been possible.

Alan Stacy, Fort Frye High School, Beverly, Ohio

Fun and Games on Mount Olympus

After a unit on mythology, my students enjoy these review games. They can, of course, be adapted to suit other literature units.

Who Am I? Pin the name of a mythological character to the back of each student without the student seeing the name. The task is to ask yes and no questions of classmates in an effort to determine the name. A student who feels ready to hazard a guess checks with me. A correct identification on the first try earns the maximum number of points, with a reduction of points for each additional guess.

Meet the Press. Students come to class dressed as mythological characters and are interviewed by other students posing as journalists. A perfect opportunity to use your school's video-cassette recorder and camera!

Mythopoly. Make large game boards out of tagboard, sectioning them off in squares similar to commercial table games. Shaking dice to determine the number of squares, players move a marker around the board. The object is to be the first player to reach the Elysian Fields. Some squares are simply safe squares on which to stop. Others have pitfalls (Cerberus and the Stymphalian Birds, for example) that require players to move back a given number of spaces. Still others offer rewards (Diana and Ceres, for example) and allow players to move forward an additional number of spaces. Finally, there are squares labeled "Fates," with accompanying cards (similar to "Chance" and "Community Chest") that bring good or bad luck to the player.

Myth-o. Students make cards modeled after Bingo cards, with names (people and places) from mythology in each square. The teacher or a student reads off descriptions of the characters or places. The students must recognize who or what is being described and cover that square if the name appears on their cards. Zeus, for example, could be described as "Father-god" or "Husband of Hera." The appropriate reward for the winner? A *Mars* bar—what else?

Mary Eberling, Sacajawea Junior High School, Federal Way, Washington

A Class to Remember

On April 14, 1912, the "unsinkable" *Titanic,* flagship of the White Star Line, on her maiden voyage from Southampton to New York, struck an iceberg and sank off the southeast coast of Newfoundland with the loss of 1503 lives.

Walter Lord's *A Night to Remember,* a minute-by-minute account of the sinking, is an excellent book for junior high school English classes.

Interesting and readable, it permits teaching strategies that cover major areas of English instruction. What follows is an outline of how I recently taught the book to eighth-graders.

General Discussion

After students had read the book, we discussed the story in general terms. I posed a number of topics for their reactions:

1. The social structure of the time, with particular reference to the "classes" on the liner

2. "Ifs" that might have changed the fate of the *Titanic* and her crew and passengers

3. The changing views of passengers as the enormity of the situation began to unfold

4. Important changes in Atlantic liner service that came about as a result of the tragedy

Individual Projects

Some of the ideas listed below occurred to me as a result of class discussions; others were suggested by students. Each student researched and wrote up a topic; later these projects were coordinated and offered as a seminar for the entire class. Occasionally two students collaborated on a topic.

1. Investigate another disaster: the crash of the *Hindenburg,* the sinking of the *Lusitania,* the crash of Air New Zealand's Flight 901 into Mt. Erebus, the collapse of the Vancouver Second Narrows Bridge, the destruction of the oil drilling platform Ocean Ranger, the Halifax explosion in 1917.

2. Use local or national newspaper files to research the reporting of the *Titanic*'s sinking. If your students have access to the *New York Times* for April 15–19, 1912, they will be fascinated with the day-by-day coverage.

3. Read another account of the *Titanic* story and report to the class. Among your choices: H. W. Baldwin, *Admiral Death: Twelve Adventures of Men against the Sea* (1939); Lawrence Beesley, *The Loss of the SS Titanic* (1973); G. J. Marcus, *The Maiden Voyage* (1969); Wyn C. Wade, *The Titanic: End of a Dream* (1979).

4. Read Clive Cussler's novel *Raise the Titanic* and report to the class.

5. Two poems based on the *Titanic*'s sinking are Thomas Hardy's "The Convergence of the Twain" and E. J. Pratt's "The *Titanic*." Read these and "teach them" to the class.

6. Read the *Search for the Titanic* by William Hoffman and Jack Grimm and discuss the 1980 and 1981 quests for the *Titanic*.

7. Discuss contemporary problems with icebergs and the threat they pose in the North Atlantic, particularly to oil and gas rigs operating in the Hibernia field off Newfoundland.

Additional Activities

1. Transform the classroom into a Panel of Inquiry investigating the circumstances surrounding the *Titanic* disaster. Some students take the role of panel commissioners and others testify before the commission.

2. Writing assignment: Pretend that you are a *Titanic* survivor. Explain how you came to be on the vessel. Describe the sinking and your rescue by the *Carpathia*.

3. It may be possible, especially in metropolitan areas, to arrange an interview with a *Titanic* survivor. Such an interview, conducted by two members of my eighth-grade class, provided an exciting climax to our study of *A Night to Remember*.

James Satterthwaite, Point Grey Secondary School, Vancouver, British Columbia

Virtue: Prospect and Retrospect

After students have read the section of Benjamin Franklin's autobiography that deals with his attempt to attain the thirteen virtues, we discuss the mores, morals, and attitudes of Franklin's time and compare them with those of contemporary society. As a follow-up assignment, students write a paper, using first person, in which they list three virtues they feel they need to acquire or strengthen. A part of the paper should specify how these virtues may be acquired within the framework of their lives.

I file away these papers and at the end of the school year ask students to reread them and write a paragraph in which they summarize how well they did with their attempts at virtue.

Sandra Gray, Central High School, San Angelo, Texas

One, Two, Three—Testing

In lieu of an oral or written book report, I sometimes ask students to devise an exam for the book they have read. If another student reads one of these books, he or she may elect to take the test for a bonus grade. The assignment goes something like this.

1. Write an examination with an answer key for the book you read. The exam should include a short-answer section and an essay section.
2. Include ten true and false, ten multiple choice, and ten matching questions in the short-answer section.
3. The essay section should contain three questions. Consider theme, plot, setting, and characterization when you devise these questions.
4. Be sure the directions for taking the test are clear.
5. The key should include answers to short-answer questions and an answer in outline form for each of the essay questions.

Clifford Milo, Pomona Junior High School, Suffern, New York

Author IDs

The scope of the chronological literature survey in a high school English course is necessarily limited. By allotting specific responsibility to students for comprehensive information on assigned authors, I've been able to achieve fuller coverage and benefits shared by all. Here's how the system works.

Students draw a card from a stack of author cards. Thus they are "born" as authors. Their task thereafter is to know themselves—what they think about, do, try to do, write about. Students promptly complete sufficient superficial research to fill out both sides of author ID cards that resemble the one below. They go on to read a substantial sample of their authors' works (two novels or the equivalent), biographical materials, and representative criticism.

```
                                                        side one
    Name:

    My best-known works:

    My vocation:

    My avocation:

    In writing my intent is

    One or more threads that run through my work:


```

```
                                                    side two
My close friends and fellow artists:

Influences in my life and works:


I am a part of the _____ movement, the
principles of which are


Comments of critics who review and analyze my work:
```

I encourage students to "speak" for their authors whenever a theme or point of view or symbol under discussion suggests a connection. An allusion to Cain encountered while the class is reading *Beowulf,* for example, might trigger a comment on Claudius's prayer from the student who "is" Shakespeare and who is prereading *Hamlet.* When the class reads Ben Jonson's touching poem "On My First Son," the student who is Wordsworth might preview the Lucy poems. Making connections such as these gives students the comfortable recognition that writers deal with experiences common to the human condition, no matter what the century.

I urge students to identify as completely as possible: to speak in their author's voice, to use the author's words when possible, to imagine themselves to be in the author's time and place—to dress, to eat, to travel, to listen to the music of the period, to react to the news of the day as that author would. To do this, students immerse themselves in the author's writing, read a biography, and review major criticism of the author's work.

Jeanne G. Howes, Atlantic Community High School, Delray Beach, Florida

Draw Me a Poem

In contemporary society, students need to be literate in a variety of "languages"—the language of print, to be sure, but also the language of symbol (math, music, computer science) and the language of the icon (art, architecture, film). Proficiency in each of these languages can be an aid to greater proficiency in the others.

Still, English teachers frequently assume that visual literacy is irrelevant to their classrooms and may actually interfere with the achievement of

high levels of literary literacy. They may recognize the value of a structured overview in teaching reading, but they seldom apply this technique
to works of literature. Such a view of a literary work, however, can help
students to discover form and purpose, to organize "information" (factual, emotional, aesthetic), to discover the writer's voice (tone, psychological distance). It can help students to appreciate the writer's craft and to
discover the writer's meaning.

I've found great value in asking students to visualize literary structure.
After reading a literary selection, I ask them to *diagram* the selection, to
put the work into some kind of visual model. I leave these instructions
open-ended to see what students come up with. Their diagrams take
many forms: a central conflict between or within a character (perhaps
color-coded), the major structural pattern of a work (as the linear, repeti-
tive, interlocking pattern of *Canterbury Tales*), the relationship of a work
to its setting.

Less able students may need help, but ideas are contagious and students soon "see" what they are after. Exceptionally able students may
well come up with very sophisticated ideas relating disciplines; students in
one class structured *Murder in the Cathedral* in the form of a Vivaldi
mass. One caution: The end product of this assignment is not an illustration of the work but a diagram of it.

Marjorie Lieneck, Hastings High School, Hastings-on-Hudson, New York

Swift, the Stuldbruggs, and the Question of Immortality

I ask students to jot down three wishes, the anything-is-possible, fairy-
godmother type. They enjoy thinking about impossibilities and are attentive when I collect the lists—no names attached—and read the wishes
aloud. Usually at least one student lists "living forever," and that allows
me to open up the discussion of immortality. It's interesting to note that
many students adamantly favor mortality because they are concerned
about being bored. At this point I tell those skeptics that Swift agreed
and dealt with the idea in *Gulliver's Travels*. Then I assign chapter ten,
Part Three.

After we've finished the reading, we discuss Gulliver's lesson and
Swift's message. Most agree that if the Stuldbruggs are the prototype,
they're glad to be mortal.

The writing assignment that follows combines literary analysis with
opinion. I put it something like this: "Imagine a Council of Guardian
Angels assembled to choose a small number of human beings to be
granted immortality. Your name has come up, and your guardian angel
has been summoned. You must write a letter for your angel to take

along, expressing why you would or would not like to be one of the immortals and what policy the angels should adopt in making their choices. Support your view by referring to *Gulliver's Travels,* paraphrasing and incorporating direct quotes." Several students chose immortality and relied heavily on Gulliver's naive pre-Stuldbruggian ideal, which was fine as long as they dealt with the Stuldbruggs as well.

I've found this assignment a good one to do along with my students. They are very interested in hearing each other's opinions—and mine too—and the logic behind them. In turn, I am amazed at their insight into the big questions of life and death.

Rebecca A. Stiff, Stevensville High School, Stevensville, Montana

Tests That Begin After They're Taken

This activity is designed to help students think critically about the answers to essay questions. Students deal not only with their own answers but also with the answers of their classmates and with a theoretically "perfect" answer. The activity also moves the responsibility for learning in the student's direction. My social studies teaching mate and I used this idea with sixty gifted eighth-graders, and we plan to use it with our regular eighth-graders soon. Our immediate goal was to test whether our students had read an assigned text, *Animal Farm,* so we gave the test before discussing the book in class, but the activity could also be used as a follow-up to the study of a book or as a review exercise. The procedure we followed is summarized below.

1. Assign each student to a group. We had ten groups of six students each. Write an essay test with the same number of questions as you have groups. Formulate questions that require students to pull together several pieces of evidence from the text. The answers must be fairly short and straightforward, but at the same time they should require synthesis.

2. Each student takes the test.

3. Divide the class into the assigned groups and designate one question from the test to each group. Each group then writes an answer to that question. Group members freely consult with each other in composing this "perfect" answer.

4. Each group presents the answer to its question to the class. Class members may argue to add, take away, or alter parts of the answer.

5. Divide the class's test papers among the groups. Each group reads and discusses *all answers to its question,* comparing each answer with the "perfect" answer they have written. Group One, therefore,

looks only at the answer to question 1 on each test, evaluates it, and awards it a numerical score. On our test, each question was worth 10 points, so students scored each question on a scale of 0 to 10. Keep the papers rotating from group to group until all questions on all papers have been scored.

6. Return the evaluated papers to their owners who tally their scores.

Although no problems were caused by having names on the test papers, students might feel more comfortable if they were assigned numbers and remained anonymous as test-takers. We also allowed students who felt their papers had been evaluated unfairly to appeal their scores in writing to us. Each group developed its own style of evaluating answers, and we did not interfere. No problems seemed to result. The entire activity, including forty-five minutes for taking the test, was completed in two fifty-minute class periods. We felt the time was well spent, for taking the test was only the beginning of the learning experience.

Roger P. Green, Rocky Run Intermediate School, Chantilly, Virginia

2 Assignment Assortment for Writers

Teachers, like their students, spend long hours thinking about writing—what to write about and how to go about writing. Although the what and the how of writing, its content and forms, can never be separated, each of the activities in this chapter has as its central focus a challenging writing assignment. The range is great—from recasting the adventure of Little Red Riding Hood as a news story to churning out an episode for the soaps, from reacting to a doodle to responding to a painting. Implicit in each, however, is the recognition that creating a writing assignment that works is an art. The time spent in front of the desk defining and refining the assignment is ultimately as important as the time spent behind the desk grading it. The section ends with six ideas for the writing of poetry.

Eatonville Logger Rescues Child and Grandmother

Most teachers are familiar with the inverted pyramid and its role in newswriting: most important and recent information comes first. The rest follows in order of decreasing importance. In addition, I ask students to keep in mind these general principles.

1. Newswriting is objective. Don't give your opinion about events.
2. Write in the third person; use names and third-person pronouns (he, she, they). Never use second person (you) or first person (I, we). Third person is appropriate to the objective style of newswriting and does not confuse the reader.
3. Always provide attribution (sources) so that the reader can evaluate the credibility of the information.
4. Avoid opening a news story with a direct quote. Such a lead may turn away readers because it delays the story and asks them to make deductions or figure things out. If the information has been gathered in the form of direct quotations, reword them so that they appear as indirect quotations.
5. Keep sentences and paragraphs in a news story short.
6. Do not write an ending to a news story. When space runs short in a newspaper, magazine, or broadcast, the end of the story is cut first (from the bottom up). A closing will probably never appear, even if one was written.

As a practice exercise I ask students to apply these principles in casting a familiar tale as a news story. Here's how Little Red Riding Hood's story hit the wires.

> An Eatonville logger rescued a 9-year-old girl and her grandmother yesterday near Spanaway after they had been swallowed by a wolf.
>
> The girl, Little R. R. Hood, and her grandmother, Granny Hood, were listed in satisfactory condition at Lakewood General Hospital after the logger had surgically removed them from the wolf's abdomen, using his axe as a scalpel.
>
> "I just felt something wasn't right," said Paul Bunyon, 34, of Eatonville. Bunyon was driving north on Mountain Highway when he noticed the Hood's front door was open. "I couldn't believe my eyes," said Bunyon. "That wolf's stomach was bulging."
>
> Bunyon reported hearing two voices crying, "Let us out! Let us out!" He then used his axe to slice open the wolf's stomach. The girl and her grandmother stepped out. They suffered from teeth marks and slight abrasions.
>
> According to Pierce County Deputy Sheriff M. A. Copp, the girl had been delivering cookies to her grandmother when the attack occurred. The sheriff's report indicates that the wolf swallowed the grandmother and then attempted to impersonate her.
>
> "I thought it was Granny!" said the girl. "But she had such big eyes, ears, and teeth. I should have known," sobbed the child while being questioned.
>
> Copp said no charges would be filed. The wolf's body was taken to the University of Washington Medical Laboratories for rabies testing.
>
> The girl's chocolate chip cookies were recovered undamaged.
>
> Granny Hood has lived in the area for 40 years. Her granddaughter had been bringing her cookies every weekend for the past three months.

Irene Hicks, Bethel High School, Spanaway, Washington

Keys to Composition

You'll need the recording "Ebony and Ivory" by Paul McCartney and Stevie Wonder. Play it and ask students to listen attentively to the words. Play the record at least twice. Then ask students to write the meaning of the song in their own words. I think you'll be surprised by the insight most youngsters show—and by the metaphors they consciously or unconsciously develop. In essence: Keys, black and white, work together on the keyboard to create something beautiful. Why can't people, no matter what color, live together in harmony?

This technique can be used with other popular songs, especially those with a social message or those with an emotional insight particularly appealing to adolescents.

Frances B. Carter, Linkhorne Middle School, Lynchburg, Virginia

Dissertation on a Doodle

Prepare in advance a handout on which you have put the beginning of a drawing or design such as the ones shown below. Distribute the handout. Students may position the paper in any way they choose. Ask them to incorporate the lines on the handout into a drawing or design of their own. They may use the drawing on the handout as just one part of a larger, more complex drawing or they may add lines to "complete" it. Encourage them to be creative and original in their approaches. I suggest the use of color, but I also accept black and white drawings.

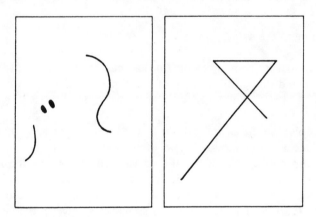

Number the pictures when they are finished, and use them in several follow-up writing assignments. You'll be surprised at how interested students are in finding out what their classmates "saw" in the handout.

1. Show selected drawings to the class and brainstorm together for words and phrases generated by a given picture. Sometimes I ask students to jot down their ideas and then share them. This tactic enables more reluctant students to contribute to brainstorming. List the words and phrases on the chalkboard or on a projector transparency, and students can draw on this idea pool in writing a reaction paragraph to a given drawing.

2. Postulate that a given picture is an illustration from a published story. From what is seen in the picture, ask for appropriate titles for the story. Again, I usually ask students to jot down one or two titles before we begin to share them. Justifying or explaining title choices is half the fun.

3. Select a completed design and ask each student to write a noun, an adjective, a verb, an adverb, and a preposition that come to mind when looking at the design. Exchange papers. Each student then writes a paragraph incorporating the words he or she received.

4. Ask each student to select a picture about which to write. The form may be descriptive or narrative, prose or poetry.

The numbering system allows more than one student to choose the same picture. It also takes care of students who may have been absent during the drawing stage of the assignment.

Ann Damerow, Northshore Junior High School, Seattle, Washington

Responding to the Arts

Asking students to respond to the fine arts can produce some of the most interesting and thoughtful writing of the semester. Here are two ways to go about it. The first is based on a response to music, the second on a response to the visual arts.

Play a piece of music and ask students to draw or paint as they listen. Artistic talent is not required, and often designs are more appropriate than drawings of people or specific scenes. Stop to discuss the kinds of drawings and the colors the music evoked. Play the selection again. This time students write freely whatever the music suggests. Ask those who are willing to share their writing. Discuss similarities between the visual and verbal responses. What qualities in the music evoked these responses? As a creative extension to this activity, ask each student to revise the writing and drawing responses and combine them in a poster.

Display a painting or project a slide of a work of art. Provide enough background about the work to place it in perspective or to relate it to a unit students are studying. Allow students a few minutes to jot down words and phrases that come immediately to mind to describe the work. Then discuss two or three questions you have formulated about the work, allowing time for students to respond to each one in writing before going on to the next. Conclude with a question that asks students to relate the work to their own lives. These responses can then become the prewriting for a more developed writing assignment.

As a follow-up, arm students with questions and send them out to view original works of art in the community: churches, statues, museum pieces, homes. Their responses can become the basis for major essays on the arts in daily life.

Theresa A. Manchey, James Wood High School, Winchester, Virginia

Picture Paragraph

I use the following individual study unit on the descriptive paragraph with ninth-graders with great success. The step-by-step procedure seems to help unenthusiastic writers. From time to time students also seem to enjoy a project that is entirely under their own management and control. Of course the handout outlined below can be modified and improved, but it's a beginning.

Individual Study: The Descriptive Paragraph

This unit of independent study will produce a descriptive paragraph of which you'll be proud—if you follow each step below. Do not try to "cut corners" or skip steps. Speed is not the important factor; work at your own pace. This does not mean you are to fool around in class; all work must be completed by everyone. On _____(date)_____, each of you will be asked to hand in the completed unit, which includes the answers *in writing* to the questions listed below, the picture of your choice, and the draft and final copy of your descriptive paragraph.

1. Find a photograph or picture that genuinely appeals to you. You must be able to cut it out and include it with your unit. Remember when you make your selection that you will share this picture with classmates.
2. Study your picture. What portion (or aspect) seems to be the most prominent? This is the central idea or image.
3. Think of a phrase that accurately and specifically describes the central idea or image. Write it down.
4. What mood or feeling dominates the picture?
5. What qualities about the picture help to create the dominant mood?
6. Keeping in mind the central idea or image and the dominant mood, decide on a title for your picture. Write it down. This title may become the title of your final paragraph.
7. Imagine that you are describing your picture for someone unable to see it. Try to convey the picture as completely as possible. Write down every one of the details that you mention to this person. For example: ducks, background trees, water, sky, mist, spring, breeze.

8. Remember that you perceive the world around you with five senses: sight, sound, smell, touch, taste. Look back at the list you made for question 7 to see how many of the senses your list of details covers. Make a revised list, one that relies on all five senses. Follow the format shown below. Some words, *mist* for example, appeal to more than one sense and may be included more than once.

sight:	ducks	sound:	quacking
	background trees		rustle of leaves
	water		lapping waves
	sky	smell:	moist air (mist)
	mist		swampy smell
touch:	breeze		of shoreline
	mist	taste:	moist air
	water		

9. What adjectives and adverbs would you add to the words and phrases in number 8 to increase clarity and appeal? Rewrite the list from number 8, adding these adjectives and adverbs. It's also a good idea to begin turning those single words into phrases— even sentences.

   ducks: ducks in silhouette circling the nearly hidden pond

   background trees: trees, freshly green, nearly hiding the pond from view

   water: still water nestled in a ring of trees

   quacking: their sharp quack pierced the silence

   breeze: the air was cool after the sudden spring storm

   moist air: the moist air clung to my skin

   swampy smell: the swampy smell of the decaying vegetation at the water's edge seemed a reminder of winter

10. Now that you have put your picture into words, you must consider whether or not you have too many details; too much detail is distracting and boring. Do you feel that any of the ideas you listed in number 9 should be excluded from the paragraph you are going to write? You want to retain reader interest, but you want to write concisely and intensely. Circle any of the details listed in step 9 that you would consider leaving out.

11. Remember your readers: attract their attention and keep it; appeal to the senses. Now you are ready to write. Convey as complete a word picture of the photograph as you can. Make clear to your readers the dominant mood or the central idea of the picture. It may help if you recall why you chose the title. Then go back to the list of details in step 9. Number them in the order in which you think you will use them in the paragraph.

12. This is the most important step! Complete the rough draft of your descriptive paragraph. Ask another student to read it; *then* show that student the picture. Discuss how to improve the paragraph. *Everyone* will have corrections to make!

13. Write a final copy on a separate sheet of paper. Check to make sure there are no silly errors. Exchange papers with a classmate and check again. Turn in your picture, your word lists, the rough draft, and the final copy. Folders for this material will be provided on the due date.

Cyril A. Haynes. Milton Williams Junior High School, Calgary, Alberta

School Mailbag

This activity engenders a delightful cooperation between primary and high school students. In our school district, the form of the letter is taught and practiced at grade two. Since receiving answers is the best possible motivation for young letter writers, we devised the following correspondence situations. As a result, second-graders are highly motivated to develop letter-writing skills, and high school students learn to adapt message to audience.

At Christmas time, second-graders write letters to Santa Claus. These are delivered to Santa's helpers (students in eleventh-grade English classes). The eleventh-graders make up names for themselves and answer each letter individually. Later in the year, we repeat the exchange with "Dear Abby, I have a problem" letters from second-graders and wise answers from high school juniors.

Marilyn West, South St. Paul Senior High School, South St. Paul, Minnesota

Fantastic!

Discuss fabulous creatures (griffins, unicorns, manticores) with the class to get imaginations going. You might bring in some bestiaries and illustrated children's books (Maurice Sendak's *Where the Wild Things Are*, for example) or sketch an add-a-line, never-never creature at the board (each student adds one element with colored chalk). After this warm-up, each student draws an imaginary animal. Important: No talking allowed and keep the drawings secret.

On a separate sheet of paper ask each student to write a paragraph or two describing the unique animal he or she has created so that someone who has never seen the animal could picture it. Assign a number to each student and ask that it be put on the drawing and on the corresponding written description. Collect the pictures and paragraphs and put the pictures aside.

Give each student a sheet of drawing paper and a paragraph written by another student. Students now draw the animals they envision from the written descriptions. Again, no talking allowed. Ask students to number their drawings to match the numbers on the paragraphs they received. Collect the paragraphs and the second set of drawings.

Display each written description with its two drawings, the original drawing and the one made on the basis of information in the written paragraph. Ideally, the two drawings should resemble each other. In practice, discrepancies will be apparent, and some lively discussion about the descriptive paragraphs will result.

Vary the game plan by trading written descriptions with students in another class. Secrecy is not required this way, but many students enjoy top-security assignments and the fun of class disclosures. Another variation: Put up *only* the second drawings and see if each student can identify the one that is *supposed* to match his or her written description.

This assignment is enjoyed by reluctant writers, but it has limitations. The descriptions tend to be rather like lists and somewhat "factual." Of course better writers are creative and incorporate figurative language, but average writers need suggestions from you if they are to avoid monotony.

Nancy Grier, Monroe School, Port Angeles, Washington

Soaps

Recently my eleventh-grade writing students developed episodes for soap operas. The assignment was a tremendous success. Students worked in groups of four or five, and while it took them a fair bit of time to churn out their episodes, the results were well worth it. What follows is a copy of the assignment I gave students.

> "The Edge of Night" has just been canceled by CBS. The network is now looking for a lively new soap opera to fill the vacant afternoon time slot. You have already sent the network a brief summary, and they have expressed interest in your work. They have asked you to submit one short episode (approximately twenty minutes in length) and to include at least two of the following items in that episode: a confession, a startling discovery, a confrontation, a reconciliation.
>
> Here is a copy of the summary you submitted to the network.
>
> Setting
> The soap takes place in Hendrikson, a small midwestern town in the United States. A famous cardiac unit is situated there, and thus doctors and researchers from all over the world come to Hendrikson. Hendrikson is also the costume jewelry capital of North America.

Characters

At sixty-three, *Dr. Ken Kerring*, director of the cardiac unit, is a trusted figure in Hendrikson and highly regarded at City Hospital. It has been ten years since his wife disappeared in a boating accident in the West Indies. Strangely enough, Mrs. Kerring's body was never found.

Shirley Brooks has recently come to Hendrikson. The daughter of Dr. Kerring's "black sheep" brother, Shirley grew up on a tropical island, where she contracted a rare disease. The disease is fatal, but Shirley knows nothing about it. Only Dr. Kerring knows the truth.

Worthington Malcolm has recently become engaged to Shirley Brooks. He has just taken over the management of the large international jewelry firm founded by his father, with whom he does not get along.

Melissa Malcolm-Newton, Worthington's young sister, has been kidnapped twice—by two different groups of terrorists—in the past year. As a result, she has lost her memory and does not recognize her husband, Dr. Jonathan Newton. Jonathan has recently become interested in Jane Cashin, a patient at his clinic.

N.B. Be sure to submit a covering letter with your soap opera episode.

Mary Ellen Selby, Templeton Secondary School, Vancouver, British Columbia

Futures: Fantasy and Fact

This writing assignment fits nicely into a unit on career education and is intended for twelfth-graders who have no particular postsecondary educational goals. With modification, of course, it can be used in other ways and with other students. This is the assignment sheet I distribute.

1. Pretend you have been given the power to see yourself ten years from now. Describe in writing your future as you wish it to be, as it could be if all your problems were gone. We'll call this description "romantic." Remember, you have the power to see whatever you wish.

2. You still have the power to describe what your life will be like ten years from now, but this time you must write a *realistic* description. You must show what it will really be like, not what you wish it could be. Remember, write what you really believe will happen.

3. You now have two descriptions—one romantic, one realistic. Read them carefully. For almost all people, the two are quite different. Try to answer these questions about your two views.
   a. What differences do you see in these descriptions? List them.
   b. How do you feel about the differences you see between your romantic and realistic future? Write an honest reaction.

    c. What can you do about the way you feel? List steps you can
       take to find a sensible compromise between your romantic
       notion and your realistic view.

This writing assignment makes two assumptions about students. One, they have competence; they have a global ability to think, imagine, write, and assess. Two, they can bring this ability to bear on the assignment without receiving direct instruction. This assignment also assumes that the teacher will examine the written products and help students improve them, via revision or by transfer to subsequent assignments.

Ronald J. Goba, Hingham Public Schools, Hingham, Massachusetts

The Door

This fifty-minute, in-class writing/revision exercise stimulates creativity and encourages students to make vivid, precise word choices. If you like, it can be extended to a three-day sequence: draft, revise, share. I begin by shutting the door to the classroom and writing two leads on the board:

    When I walk out that door, I want . . .

    When I walk out that door, I don't want . . .

I suggest a frame of mind: "Write whatever in your wildest imagination you don't want to see or do when you leave this room and then what more than anything in the world you want to see or have happen to you when you walk out that door at the end of the hour." I don't talk about revision at this point or mention that we may read some of these adventures aloud. I don't want students to worry about the final product in the early stages of its development.

After about twenty minutes, I ask students to stop and rewrite, improving verbs first. I encourage them to look for particular qualities of emotion, shades of meaning; *dash*, for example, instead of *went*. Then they repeat the process for nouns and modifiers.

At this point I ask students to exchange papers, to underline what they consider to be the most effective word choices in the paper, and to indicate the overall impression the words convey. Do they seem melancholy, wistful, vigorous, cheerful, dreamy?

Finally, time permitting, I ask volunteers to read whole paragraphs, selected sentences, or favorite words only. Then the rest of us try to guess the tone of the piece—delight, anxiety, panic, tranquility.

Thomas Lavazzi and Laura Mitchell, Southwest Missouri State University, Springfield, Missouri

Fight in Room 209!

For the past three years, Fred Zirm, my friend and fellow English teacher, and I have team taught a journalism unit. The two-week unit has three segments: opinion pieces (editorials, reviews, consumer reports), people/ event articles (reports on dances, athletic events, and the like), and special features (art, horoscopes, puzzles). Here is how we handle one exercise from the people and events section.

One of us begins an introduction of the unit, explaining the expectations we have for the class and outlining the first assignment. Then, on cue, I begin harassing Fred, mildly at first and verbally, but finally we tussle. I grab his tie; he throws an eraser. Teasing turns to taunting. After a few minutes we stop, and students are asked to describe what they have just seen. After the shock has worn off, they spend about ten minutes writing. We then share what has been written, comparing factual details and descriptive techniques.

Next, Fred and I introduce a number of descriptive writing exercises involving setting, mood, and physical appearance. We also complete a dialogue exercise and consider how routine actions can be used to reveal character. Students turn again to the fight draft. We discuss the kinds of openings a reporter can use: action, setting, physical appearance, dialogue. Students then begin the fight scene again—and again—using each of the options. We share these experiments briefly, noting the effect created by each.

At the end of the journalism unit, students rewrite the fight scene, using as many of the techniques we covered in class as they can. The last day is a sharing of those rewrites.

We have found that the fight rewrites are among the best work our students do all year long. Since the "staged fight" is witnessed by all, it provides a common experience—and a memorable one. Then, too, students are especially attentive, given the unusual behavior of their stuffy teachers. Finally, students usually side with their own teacher during the fight and tend to use slanted language in their reports to show their allegiance. This last is an extremely valuable response, and we make use of it in two other exercises during the unit. In the first, students write to make something good sound bad and vice versa; two popular topics are Bo Derek and school lunches. In the second, students are given a list of physical characteristics. Half of the class writes a paper using these characteristics to describe a "loser"; the other half, using the same list, describes a "cool dude."

Peter Jenkins, Landon School, Bethesda, Maryland

Twenty Plus One

The following writing ideas are among those used by teachers at Westchester High, levels nine through twelve, for short journal assignments and expanded compositions.

1. Make a collage about yourself and then write about it.
2. "What if . . . ?" assignments.
3. Looking ahead to 19____, what and where do you hope to be?
4. An APB (all-points bulletin) about yourself as "Wanted," complete with picture.
5. A letter to the world to be read only after you have died.
6. The perfect friend.
7. A description of what you would put in a 10′ × 10′ room if you were to be confined there for one month (no people allowed).
8. What you would do with $10,000.
9. A description of the wedding you would like to have.
10. A description of a green pepper, an ear of corn, a tomato, and an orange for a blind person.
11. A detailed map that would get a first-grader from the front door of your high school to your home.
12. A comic strip that presents your philosophy of life.
13. The topic you would teach if you could take over in any one of your classes.
14. The most important thing you have learned about yourself this year.
15. The animal you would be and why.
16. A description of the person you most respect and an explanation of why.
17. Observations of people you like and don't like—with explanations.
18. The one thing you most want to do by the time you are twenty-five (or thirty, etc.).
19. Most disliked food—and why.
20. A poem about a picture you have found.
21. A description of yourself from your parents' point of view.

Claire Miller, Westchester High School, Houston, Texas

Garbage In, Garbage Out: The Art of Creating Writing Assignments

As any computer student knows, a computer analysis is only as reliable as the data that was programmed in. This principle is often stated rather simply: garbage in, garbage out. I believe an analogy to this critical input-output relationship exists in the devising of writing assignments. I have often spent ten hours reading, evaluating, and commenting on a set of papers, but the assignment that generated all that writing took me only ten minutes to create. Keeping in mind the computer analyst's maxim, I now dedicate more time and effort to devising assignments that will produce the best possible output.

In virtually every writing occasion at work or at home, the writer is aware of five basic components that govern the written message: *Who* is saying *what* to *whom* for what *purpose* and in what *medium*? When I formulate an assignment, I try to incorporate those five elements. Briefly, I try to include the answers to five questions.

1. Who is speaking and in what voice?
2. What is the basic information to be communicated?
3. To whom is the writer speaking (the audience)?
4. What is the purpose of this message?
5. What medium would be most effective for this message?

The following three assignments were created with those five questions in mind.

1. You are Shirley Jackson's publisher and you have received a flood of angry correspondence after printing "The Lottery." Some people say that Miss Jackson is "sick and evil" to even think of such a story and that you are just as "uncivilized" for publishing it. Write a letter to the editor of a national magazine in which you explain the value of the story. You want to make the reader see beyond the superficial interpretation of the tale.

2. You are an assistant editor at Bantam Books, and the company has decided to print a paperback edition of "The Most Dangerous Game" by Richard Connell. It is your job to write the 50-word blurb that will appear on the book jacket. Tell enough about the story to interest readers but don't reveal too much. You want to arouse curiosity and influence readers to buy the book.

3. While my class was reading Solzhenitsyn's *One Day in the Life of Ivan Denisovich*, a small town banned the book because of its "morally objectionable language." I gave the class a copy of the news story about the book banning. Each student was then asked to write a letter to that local school board. The task was to take and justify a position regarding the censorship. Regardless of the position taken, the purpose of the letter was to influence the board through persuasive argument.

Michael Graner, U.S. Coast Guard Academy, New London, Connecticut

At Fourteen, at Fifteen, at Sixteen

Following a suggestion of Phillip Lopate ("Poet's World," *Literary Cavalcade*, December 1981), try using Ezra Pound's "The River-Merchant's Wife: A Letter" as the model for a poetry-writing assignment.

After we have discussed the poem and its structure, I give the assignment, noting that the relationship described may be boy-girl but that it may be one of many other kinds, too. Students have used parents, siblings, teachers—even teddy bears. I ask them to think of a relationship they have had which changed over the years as they grew and changed. They are to describe this relationship in a poem using divisions of time similar to those in "River-Merchant's Wife." We review Pound's reliance on concrete detail and note again how each stanza shows a different stage of the relationship. The poem below resulted from that assignment.

Letter

I watched for you every day
On the long march to lunch.
My class would meet your class in
    the halls
And I would try to catch your attention,
Becoming loud and obnoxious.
You never noticed and I gave up,
Crying into my pillow.

In Junior High we fell in love
As we sat quietly on the bus.
Your long, dark hair fell over the
    seat
As we rolled on through the night.
Too shy to talk, we sat peacefully
    all the way home.

Winter came and I loved you more:
Your brown eyes and soft ways.
I could talk to you, and you to me;
We laughed and rode your horse
Across the snow-covered prairie all
    day.

And then I left, swiftly, suddenly.
I did not think I would see you
    again.
Across half a continent our letters
    traveled,
And I walked through the trees and
    dreamed of you.

I see you now, winters and summers,
But it is not the same.
We laugh and ride your horse
Across the prairie all day,
But it is not the same.
I miss you.

                        Kevin Packard

Margot M. Miller, Ketchikan High School, Ketchikan, Alaska

Ten Little Letters Standing in a Row

Don't reject this idea out of hand. It sounds gimmicky, but the results suggest that sometimes restrictions can liberate, not limit, the imagination.

Choose five letters at random; then choose five more (x, z, and q are difficult). For example: AKSCR/TBMOL. Use the first five letters as the initial letters of words in lines 1, 3, and 5 of a five-line poem; use the second five in lines 2 and 4. Words must follow the order in which the letters were originally chosen, but other words may be added. Here's an example of the products you can expect from students.

> The Formula
> AKSCR: initial letters of five words in lines 1, 3, and 5
> TBMOL: initial letters of five words in lines 2 and 4

> The Poem
> After killing a snake my brother cried and ran.
> The waves broke then and mountains frowned over long shadows
> awkward on kind shores. He cringed and remembered
> the sharp break of the mottled body. Our lake
> answered keening songs that crashed and rolled at our feet.

Robin Hamilton, Hellgate High School, Missoula, Montana

Discovery Poems

Collect in advance unusual pictures clipped from magazines. You'll need about twice as many pictures as you have students. You'll also need a recording or tape of a musical selection sung in a foreign language.

Starting from several places in the room, distribute stacks of pictures. Each student selects a picture that he or she finds appealing and passes the remaining pictures to the next person. When everyone has a picture, explain that the class is going to hear someone singing in a foreign language, which they are not expected to understand. Instead, their task is to imagine what the song is about and to relate that idea in some way to the picture each of them holds. Ask students to immerse themselves in the music and just write. Disjointed words and phrases will come at first, but gradually a more coherent pattern or idea will emerge. Encourage students to get ideas, rhythm, pattern, into flowing lines without regard to spelling or sentence construction—revision comes later.

I use East Indian music. Totally different from Western music, it seems to free imaginations to move in unpredictable directions. The kids giggle at first, but I've gotten some very interesting poems when they rework their notes.

Jean Smith, Martinsville High School, Martinsville, Virginia

A Poet behind Every Notebook

The cinquain is a five-line poem with some of the attributes of Haiku, but it holds particular promise for the I-can't-write-a-poem student. The formal and informal patterns illustrated below offer a threshold of success that frequently leads to genuine creativity. Both poems were written by students at Baker High School.

The formal cinquain is based on a syllable pattern:

> line 1: two syllables
> line 2: four syllables
> line 3: six syllables
> line 4: eight syllables
> line 5: two syllables

And here's an example of the kind of cinquain my students wrote in response to that pattern.

> The truck
> ran screaming down
> the hill. Its brakes were gone.
> I saw it end, a shuddering,
> sad wreck.

An informal cinquain can be organized on the following pattern:

> line 1: noun
> line 2: two adjectives
> line 3: three participles or three gerunds
> line 4: statement about the noun
> line 5: synonym for the noun

That pattern produced this poem.

> Cowboy
> Rough, tough
> Riding, roping, throwing
> His spurs jangle every step.
> Macho!

Eloise Dielman, Baker High School, Baker, Oregon

Four-Day Hands-on Poetry Workshop

Begin each day with selected poems or lines from poems that correlate with the poetry assignment for that day. Each idea is then explored individually by the poets (that's everybody!) in your classroom. On the following day, the poems are "published" on the bulletin board.

Day One: Colors

Lines from Emily Dickinson work well as "seed": her "silver chronicle," the "scarlet gown" in which she dresses a field, the "purple traffic" of her nights, her "molten blue." Robert Frost's "Nothing Gold Can Stay" is another fine choice, especially for high school juniors and seniors.

> *The assignment:* Write a poem with a color word or image in every line. You may incorporate many colors or limit yourself to one. Remember, there are many color-conveying words besides the names of colors: *freckled, misty, bleak, burning,* for example.

Day Two: Animals

There are so many animal poems to choose from and teachers are certain to have their own favorites. Here are a few to think about: Blake's "Lamb" and "Tiger," Tennyson's "Eagle," Frost's "Departmental," D. H. Lawrence's "Snake," Richard Wilbur's "The Death of a Toad," Richard Eberhart's "The Groundhog."

> *The assignment:* Write a poem about an animal in which you make as many accurate observations about that animal as you can. Try to show directly or indirectly how you feel about that animal.

Day Three: Apologies

Read aloud William Carlos Williams's "This Is Just to Say," the delightfully understated admission of guilt for having eaten "the plums that were in the icebox."

> *The assignment:* Remember when you did something—and you apologized but didn't really mean it? You were really, perhaps secretly, glad you had done what you had done. Write a poem apologizing for something you're really glad you did. You may also write on something you would like to do (secretly, of course) and pretend to be sorry for later.

Day Four: An Object

Put William Carlos Williams's brief "So Much Depends" on the chalkboard. Yes, that's the one with the red wheelbarrow and the white chickens.

> *The assignment:* Write a poem in which you use Williams's form. The poem is a single sentence. The line pattern, three words and then one, is repeated four times. Begin your poem as Williams did:
>
> So much depends
> upon

Lou Kister, Mead Junior High School, Mead, Washington

Poetry Windfall

Frost watched his woods fill up with snow. Emily Dickinson glimpsed the snow sifting from leaden sieves, ruffling the wrists of posts. Whittier saw a universe of sky and snow—"no cloud above, no earth below." What images will your students discover in the first snow fall?

Since the scheduled lesson plan is doomed on the day of the first snowfall, use the excitement to generate descriptive writing. We begin by observing the snow falling. Maybe I'll turn off the lights for a minute or two. Then we create a word bank of adjectives, nouns, adverbs, and verbs that seem to connect with falling snow. Simile and metaphor may be included at this step, and sometimes we appoint a thesaurus and dictionary committee to help out.

Each student then completes a piece of descriptive writing that focuses on the snow. The type is up to the individual. Among the possibilities are cinquain (a noun, two adjectives describing the noun, three verbs telling what the noun is or does, a short phrase related to the noun, a repetition of the noun or a synonym or closely related word); a 5-W poem (five lines of description, each in turn answering who or what or when or where or why, sequenced as the poet chooses); a descriptive paragraph; haiku; a concrete poem that creates a storm of words on the page.

Later, students revise in small groups or with the help of a writing partner. I encourage oral reading during the revision process. Finally, students fold and cut a large snowflake from unlined white paper, leaving a fairly solid middle section for writing or pasting the revised description.

The snowflakes are posted on a bulletin board covered with blue paper, an attractive and easy way of sharing our work with each other and with other classes.

Mary Hatcher, Glassboro Intermediate School, Glassboro, New Jersey

3 Prewriting and Polishing

Only when students are encouraged to complete the entire writing process will they be satisfied with their written products and proud to share them. Prewriting and revision are two crucial stages in that all-important process. The joy of spontaneity and the excitement of a writing high must be balanced by the responsibility and patience that produce clear as well as powerful communication. The nine activities that immediately follow relate to prewriting, the remaining half dozen to revision and editing. Of special interest are the activities that take the red pencil from the teacher's hand, at least for an interim period, and give it to student evaluators: collaborative reading, composition conversations, and revision groups. Ideas about prewriting and revision are also found as part of many of the writing assignments in chapter two.

Extemporaneously Speaking

Classes enjoy this informal prewriting assignment because it generates lots of audience involvement. It's useful early in the year because it allows students to give informal demonstration speeches without the threat of a grade. It also provides an opportunity for students to consider the needs of audience and the value of visual aids—whether speaking or writing.

Begin by listing on the board several simple activities, ones that require few props and are familiar to many: how to tie a necktie, how to tie your shoes, how to make a boat or party hat from newspaper, how to tie a square knot (slip knot, bow knot, sailor's knot). Ask who in the class can do the activities you have listed and jot down several names after each activity. Now choose the students who will give the demonstrations on the following day, demonstrations accompanied by impromptu explanations. If you have no student who knows how to perform a given activity, ask for someone who can find out how to do it before the next class period. All demonstrations must be presented then.

With help from you and others in the class, each speaker provides enough materials so that each member of the class can perform the activity as the speaker does it. You'll need, therefore, neckties, newspapers, yarn or twine—whatever the activities on your list require.

When the "speeches" are over, ask several members of the audience to demonstrate how well they learned each activity by performing it once again—this time in front of the class. Both speakers and audience readily grasp the pitfalls in explaining even the simplest procedure—and your class is ready to undertake a more formal how-to assignment, written or oral.

Nan Wampler, Worthington High School, Worthington, Ohio

Fantasy

This activity is enjoyed by students of almost any age, but it's especially useful as a morale-builder for students who have difficulty putting pen to paper or as a prewriting warm-up when the assignment will be stories.

Fold a large piece of butcher paper like a fan. On the first pleat of the fan, write the opening line for a story or ask a student to begin the tale. Pass the fan from student to student for each additional line on each consecutive pleat with this stipulation: Students may read only the line that was written just before they received the fan.

When everyone has had a chance to write, unfold the fan and share the fantasy. You'll discover some weird and wild stories, but you'll also find that some of those reluctant writers are tackling stories of their own with a smile instead of a grimace.

Leslie Evans, Kamenamena Schools, Honolulu, Hawaii

False Restrictions

I begin a writing workshop course by asking students to "free write" for at least the first week. After I feel that they have begun to trust me and to feel less intimidated about writing, I throw a curve: false restrictions.

The first restriction is the elimination of words with the letter *e*. I require students to write a story, an essay—or a continuous thought—for about fifteen minutes; during that time, words containing the letter *e* do not exist. Students may not misspell to eliminate the forbidden letter. When the time is up, students write without restriction for another fifteen minutes.

The next day follows the same pattern, except that words with the letter *s* are forbidden.

What do false restrictions accomplish? In the first place, they seem to generate a sense of self-hearing for beginning writers. But perhaps of greater importance, students suddenly realize that they have more thoughts than they can write and more words at their command than they thought they had. The unspoken but demonstrated conclusion: there's always *something* to write about. If you're not convinced, try it yourself. Alternative ideas crowd in, new directions suggest themselves, and another word is always at hand.

Lee Nott, Union High School, Rimersburg, Pennsylvania

Write Your Way Out of This One

These writing assignments are idea initiators and begin the process toward a revised and edited product. They are not, therefore, to be graded as finished products. I write with my students and share what I've written at the end of each writing period. Sharing my writing can be intimidating, but sharing also fosters trust.

1. You're a reporter for a large newspaper and have been granted a private interview with the movie star of your dreams. During the interview, you receive a phone call. A mysterious voice tells you that this movie star is going to be assassinated and when. What will you do? (Go to the proper authorities and get protection for the star? Keep quiet, be in on the assassination, and make a fortune by being the first reporter on the scene and the last person to see the star alive? Get a fellow reporter and try to foil the plot?) Explain your behavior.

2. In the yard of an abandoned farmhouse stands a series of gravestones that read as follows:

Jacob Thomas	Elizabeth Thomas	Jacob Thomas, Jr.
1888–1913	1881–1910	1902–1962
Shanon Thomas	Sharon Thomas	Joshua Thomas
1903–1913	1903–1913	1904–1913

   Calculate ages, estimate relationships, and describe what you think happened. How did each person die? Illness? A crazed multiple murder? A fire?

3. Create a travel brochure for a make-believe city, country, or planet. Include illustrations from magazines or drawings of your own to depict what this place would look like if it were real. Provide intriguing descriptions of all that will be found there (recreational activities, employment opportunities, educational facilities, historical buildings, local customs and foods, natural scenery).

4. You're home alone in bed when you hear a noise. All your childhood fears return. Is something in the house? You try to dismiss the thought, but your mind keeps inventing new and frightening possibilities. Where is that noise coming from? Describe what might be lurking in the house. What will happen if you get out of bed?

Terry Cooper, Inchelium School, Inchelium, Washington

Composition Conversations

For every writing assignment, I ask students to engage in a conversation with a classmate. Their conversation should be an encouraging give-and-take, the kind of supportive communication that will help them clarify and develop their ideas.

Conversation requires a speaker and a listener, and each student assumes both roles during the class sessions devoted to composition conversation. To prevent the confusion that sometimes occurs when two people have a lot to tell each other at the same time, one student does most of the talking during the first half of the period and the other does most of the listening/commenting. When the conversation ends, the speaker is given five minutes to jot down what may be helpful in composing later on. During the second half of the period, the roles are reversed.

To help students prepare for these conversational sessions, I use the following handout.

> *The speaker's role.* Come prepared to talk about your topic. Although you should *not* bring a written composition to read aloud, you might want to bring an organized list of your main ideas. As a speaker, think of your responsibilities as follows:
>
> 1. Choose your ideas wisely; don't be vague.
> 2. Provide sensible organization; don't be scatterbrained.
> 3. Speak in a manner appropriate to your partner.
>
> *The listener's role.* Listening is a complex process, and it cannot be directly observed. Think of your responsibilities as follows:
>
> 1. Pay close attention; avoid mental wandering.
> 2. Take an active, inquiring interest; avoid a "ho-hum" attitude.
> 3. Be open-minded, alert to your own biases.
> 4. Listen especially for the speaker's central ideas and their supporting evidence.
>
> All genuine communication relies on feedback, responses that indicate how successfully the message is getting across. For the purposes of these conversations, the goal of the listener is to provide as much encouragement as possible so that the speaker will continue to discuss his or her ideas. To accomplish this, highlight what is good about what the speaker is saying. Indicate your interest in the following ways:
>
> 1. Employ body language: nodding and smiling, for example.
> 2. Offer words of understanding: "Yes," "Good," "All right," "Uh-huh."
> 3. Ask for more information: "Can you clarify that?" "I'm not sure I understand." "Can you tell me again?" "And then?"
>
> The listener should make these kinds of responses throughout the conversation, and the speaker should understand that they are

intended for his or her benefit. Although they may seem artificial at first, they will make the conversation more pleasurable and useful.

All in all, participating in composition conversations will give you a powerful extra in making your writing more effective. This procedure uses talents that are fairly well developed—speaking and listening—to fuel the talent of writing. Composition, then, will become for you another means of real communication.

William H. Blanchard, Prince George's Community College, Largo, Maryland

Instructive Instructions

The following prewriting activity can be used to introduce writing assignments on directions and instructions. It's also an activity that can open discussion on the importance of specific and accurate language.

Make copies of two figures such as the one shown below. Label one figure *a* and the other figure *b*. Divide the class into an even number of small groups, for example, six groups of four students each. Give three groups copies of figure a and three groups copies of figure b.

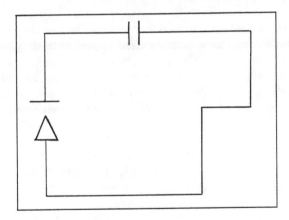

Each group then writes a set of instructions for reproducing the figure it has been given. After ten or fifteen minutes, each figure-a group exchanges instructions with a figure-b group. The figures are *not* passed along with the instructions.

Each group then attempts to reproduce the figure from the written instructions it received. After a reasonable time, the figures are distributed and each group compares its efforts with the desired end product.

Reassemble the class for a discussion of the results. What problems were encountered? Which sentences caused communication failures and which were effective in achieving the desired result? Can students provide reasons for their successes and failures?

Kathleen A. Hoeltzel, Peru High School, Peru, New York

Obtaining an Honest Writing Sample

At the beginning of the school year, I want a writing sample from each student for diagnostic purposes. I used to have trouble getting samples of more than a few sentences until I began using this topic: "You may write a poem, a letter, a story, a newspaper report; use any form you feel is appropriate. But, whatever you do, fib! The entire composition is to be one outrageous fabrication—the wilder, the better."

Using this topic, I routinely receive papers that are one to three pages in length. There is no problem persuading students to share their writing with classmates, either.

Jeff Golub, Shelton High School, Shelton, Washington

Beginning at the Beginning

Here are three strategies to show students the functions of an introduction and to enable them to write more effective and interesting introductions.

Strategy one. Ask each student to bring at least one magazine to class. In class each student selects an introduction to a magazine article that he or she finds interesting. We read our choices aloud and discuss why these introductions caught our eye. We generally conclude that they have devices to catch the reader but that they also indicate what the article is going to be about. Next we list the techniques used to hook readers: question, descriptive details, narration, comparison/contrast, shocking statement, dialogue. Finally we classify these introductions by the techniques their authors used. Each student then chooses one of these techniques and uses it to write an introduction.

Strategy two. I prepare in advance a handout on which are listed several beginnings. Students read through these and jot down what they think the next few sentences might be. We read our ideas aloud and discuss why we took off in certain directions and not in others—although we by no means have consensus about what should follow each introduction. Then we go back over the introductions, searching for clues about what is to follow. Finally, we discuss what makes these introductions interesting (gets a character or situation in front of the reader fast, makes the reader wonder what happened prior to the introduction or what will happen next, relates an unfamiliar subject to one with which the reader is familiar).

Strategy three. I write several cliché topics on the board (my summer vacation, my high school, parents, teachers, my pet) and ask students to write a brief introduction to one of them. We read some of these introductions aloud and then review the successful techniques we had discovered earlier. Each student then writes a second introduction to the same topic, and we share and critique these efforts. Then it's back to the drawing board for a third try at writing an introduction to the topic. Finally, we evaluate all three efforts, picking our favorites and justifying our choices.

Kathleen D. Andrasick, Lolani School, Honolulu, Hawaii

Tasteful Writing

Those of us who teach at the secondary level and see our students at most sixty minutes a day seem never to get to know them as well as their elementary teachers did. For this reason, I developed a writing assignment that is inherently fun, but more important, one that gives me a special insight into my students. This informal, not-for-grades assignment may be used on Valentine's Day or as Easter approaches. Sometimes I use both occasions to get to know my students better.

Decorate a valentine box like those your students enjoyed way back in elementary school. Inside place valentine suckers or another treat, but attach to each a valentine-related question that the student must answer in an informal essay. Each student reaches inside the box and selects a treat; then he or she answers the question that came with the treat. These are typical of the questions I use.

1. If you could, what would you choose to give your mother (father, other relative) besides the usual valentine gifts?
2. We associate hearts with Valentine's Day. What has been the most heart-touching experience you have had lately?
3. If you could have the valentine gift of your choice today, what would it be and why?
4. Pretend you are a valentine gift. What are you? To whom will you be given and why?
5. Valentines are usually given as an expression of love. Name one person to whom you wish you could show more love. Explain why. If you wish, you may answer this question without giving the name of the person.
6. The symbol of Valentine's Day is a heart. If you could, whose heart would you like to see into and why?
7. Who in your life so far has been a true valentine to you?
8. If you could give the world a valentine, what would you give and why?

9. Pretend that you are baking a large valentine cake for someone you like—or for someone you don't particularly care for. What surprise would you put inside the cake?

10. If your heart were visible for others to see, what would you want us to see? Why?

This writing experience is similar to the one above, but this time you provide an Easter basket with plastic eggs into which you have put candy along with a question that students answer in writing.

1. On Easter, we usually put on our best, finest appearance. What would you like to change about your appearance and why?

2. Now that spring is here, we can look back on the long winter. What are some good memories that you have about this past winter?

3. Easter is a time of rebirth. If you could be reborn in time and place, who would you be and why?

4. Should children be told there is an Easter bunny? Why or why not?

5. Holidays are usually a time for family gatherings. Describe the relative you would most like to come for Easter. Tell why you want that person to come.

6. The Easter bunny sometimes brings big surprises. What surprise would you like the bunny to bring you and why?

7. When the bell rings at the end of school today, spring vacation begins. What are some of the things you are looking forward to doing?

8. Now that spring is here, what are you most anxious to do that you could not do in winter?

9. Easter is traditionally a time of new beginnings. What about you or your life would you like to begin anew this spring?

10. If you were to give someone a plastic egg containing a treasured gift, to whom would you give it and what would be the gift?

Rosanna Reaser, Mercer County Schools, Princeton, West Virginia

The Three Bears and the Four Sentence Types

I use this exercise for promoting sentence variety with small groups of students and an overhead projector. It can, of course, be done as an individual assignment.

Divide the class into six groups and give each group a copy of the version of "The Three Bears" shown below. Each group also needs a transparency sheet for the overhead projector and a pen. Instruct each group to rewrite an assigned paragraph of the story, combining and revising sentences so that the paragraph has a variety of sentence types—

if possible one simple, one compound, one complex, and one compound-complex sentence. Students also label and punctuate the sentences.

I collect the sheets and project each paragraph in order on the screen so that the class can check sentence variety and punctuation. We also discuss how successful students have been with clause construction and sentence rhythm. When the paragraph analyses are complete, we read the revision in its entirety and compare it to the original.

The Three Bears

Once upon a time there were three bears. There was a mother bear, a father bear, and a baby bear. The three bears lived in the forest. The forest was dark. The forest was big. One day the bears decided to go out for a walk before breakfast. Their porridge was too hot. The bears left the house. They left their bowls of porridge on the table to cool.

Goldilocks was a cute little girl. Goldilocks had long golden hair. She was walking in the forest one day. She was alone. Goldilocks came upon the bears' home. The bears' home was vacant. The door was open. She walked through the door. Goldilocks didn't knock.

Goldilocks went into the kitchen. She saw three bowls of porridge. The bowls of porridge were on the table. One bowl was large. One bowl was middle-sized. One bowl was small. Goldilocks picked up a spoon. Goldilocks tasted the porridge from the small bowl. The porridge tasted good. Suddenly Goldilocks realized how hungry she was. Her long walk had given her an appetite. Goldilocks ate all the porridge from the small bowl.

Goldilocks went into the living room. She saw three chairs in the living room. One chair was large. One chair was middle-sized. One chair was small. Goldilocks sat in the small chair. The small chair broke into a hundred pieces. Goldilocks found herself on the floor. The hundred pieces scattered all over the floor.

Goldilocks went upstairs. The bedroom was upstairs. She saw three beds in the bedroom. One bed was large. One bed was middle-sized. One bed was small. Goldilocks tested the small bed. Goldilocks climbed into the small bed. The small bed was comfortable. Goldilocks felt sleepy from her long walk in the forest. Goldilocks went to sleep in the small bed.

The three bears came home. The bears had been walking in the woods. The three bears went into the kitchen. The baby bear discovered that his porridge had been eaten. The baby bear was unhappy. The three bears went into the living room. The baby bear discovered that his chair had been broken. The baby bear was unhappy. The three bears went upstairs. The baby bear discovered Goldilocks. Goldilocks was asleep in his bed. Goldilocks woke up. Goldilocks saw the bears. The bears were shocked to see her. She was shocked to see them. Goldilocks screamed and ran home. Goldilocks was frightened. She could be safe at home.

Carole B. San Miguel, J. Frank Dobie High School, Houston, Texas

Getting the Cart Back behind the Horse

The experts conclude (and I agree) that there is little transfer from successfully completed exercises in grammar books to student writing. One bridge I've discovered is to reverse the method. I don't believe this is an original idea (it's far too simple and logical to be one of my own); however, I don't remember how I came by it. I've used it for years with different types of writing and with students at different ability levels.

Reserve twenty or thirty minutes for in-class writing. Keep the assignment fairly simple but with enough substance to yield about a page of interesting writing. Collect the papers. Read through them if you want, but make no marks on them.

Return these papers to their owners after two or three days have passed and students have forgotten the details of what they have written. Ask students to copy each sentence in the composition, skipping two lines between each and numbering the sentences so that they look like an exercise out of the grammar book.

Students then examine each isolated sentence to determine if it is grammatically correct and well constructed. When sentences have been corrected or restructured, they are viewed in sequence to determine their relationships to each other and the need for transition or subordination. When the exercise is completed, the paper may be reconstructed with the revised sentences and submitted for a grade.

This exercise allows me to read the final composition without stopping to mark grammar errors (there should be none!), and my grading focuses on composition skills. The exercise also helps me to establish that editing includes examining each sentence and that the time taken to do this improves a composition (and its grade) considerably. Additionally, I am able to give instruction in grammar as a related skill to composition. Finally, I obtain useful mileage out of a single assignment without spending additional time marking papers.

Julia S. Nichols, Craigmont High School, Memphis, Tennessee

Peer Revision with Fourth- through Eighth-Graders

The single best idea for improving student writing that we have ever implemented is the use of revision groups of about five students. We started with the model set forth by Peter Elbow in *Writing without Teachers* (Oxford University Press, 1975) but quickly found that his procedures for making comments were too complicated for our students. The directions we give in a student handout are summarized below.

Reading a Paper

1. Everyone must have pencil and paper.
2. An author reads his or her paper. *No* introductory explanations or apologies are permitted.
3. The other members of the group listen quietly. When the author has finished, they jot down words or phrases with a sign beside them: A plus means "I liked it." A minus means "I didn't like it." A question mark means "I was confused by it."
4. The author now reads the paper a second time. Again the other members of the group write down words or phrases that strike them positively or negatively.

Commenting on a Paper

1. Each member of the group reads from his or her notes in turn. The others *only* listen.
2. Each commentator begins with a *positive* statement about something he or she liked in the paper.
3. At the end of his or her comments, the student states what the composition is about—*as he or she understands it.*
4. The author takes notes on his or her paper, underlining specific words or phrases and marking them with the appropriate symbol. The author may not interrupt to argue or explain.

When we introduce the idea of revision groups, we take one class session to demonstrate the process. With the whole class acting as a single group, we comment on the student comments and check their notes. After that introduction, the groups of five students meet weekly. We sit with a different group each week, but we collect all student notes to be sure they are based on direct quotes from the compositions.

We think there are two keys to the splendid success of revision groups. First, they focus the author on the audience's perception of what has been written. Second, the procedure forces students to be specific about the exact words used and their effect. Other, more general benefits seem to be improved oral reading and listening skills, refined critical abilities, improved personal communication and social skills, and the granting of a higher status to writing as an important skill.

Susan Stillman, Barbara Jordan, and Ron Cohen, Evergreen School, Seattle, Washington

Guess Who's Coming to Dinner?

As a teacher trained to judge language usage with more neutrality than is often found in traditional handbooks, I am uneasy about dictating usage to students. Many of the "errors" that handbooks deal with center around debated rules of "standard" formal usage. Consider these examples:

a. Everyone found *their place* at the table.
b. The government *have* set up new policies.
c. He's bigger than *me*.
d. *Who* did you speak *to*?
e. There was no way to get *thru* the crowd.

I realize the history and logic behind these "errors." I know that (a) is logical though inconsistent, considering the plural meaning of *everyone,* and that (b) is even acceptable British usage. I recognize that (c) and (d) represent the continuation of some old trends in the history of the language and that (e) is a logical spelling often used in informal writing but condemned in formal papers. None of these is yet accepted in the standard English of academics or the conservative language of business. Even though I may no longer believe in these rules of usage, I also realize that my employers—the taxpayers, the parents, the future employers of my students, the public—expect me to teach them to students. So I like to use this exercise based on a simple analogy to help students see usage rules not as absolute laws but as social conventions with social consequences. In fact, it's their realization of the social consequences of breaking usage rules that may motivate them to conquer and remember the rules outside my classroom.

I begin with a little pop quiz on usage rules based on examples similar to the ones cited above. At the bottom of the page I ask students to draw a picture of a "proper" place setting at the table. In the course of discussing the "correct" answers to the quiz, I ask several students to draw their table settings on the chalkboard. Some have trouble—others know the proper positions even of the bread plate and dessert spoon. I ask how many of them set the table in the proper way at home. Most admit that they don't bother unless they have company. We compare ways of setting the table for various guests—the next-door neighbor, a sister or brother, a boyfriend invited to dinner for the first time, the boss, the pastor, the mayor, President Reagan. I ask them whether it *really* does matter which side of the plate the fork and napkin go on—or which side a corsage is worn on—or whether they wear black to a funeral (remembering that white is worn for funerals in some cultures). We discuss what conventions are and the relative importance of various social—and grammatical—conventions and how conventions change through the years (like wearing hats and gloves and using *who* and *whom*). We talk about who decides what the rules are. It is my hope that this exercise gives students a more realistic idea of where grammar conventions come from and helps them realize that the importance of following such conventions depends on the person for whom they are setting the table—or writing the paper.

Derise Wigand, Washington State University, Pullman, Washington

Punctuation as Traffic Signal

When reading students' papers, I have always tried to focus first on content, next on organization or form, and finally on correctness. After all, what good is a mechanically correct paper if the content is trivial? The opposite, however, is also true: what good is a thoughtful piece of writing if incorrect mechanics interfere with the reading of the paper? In particular of late I sense—and many of my colleagues agree—that students have taken to "creative punctuation" because they do not understand the conventions of standard punctuation.

I wanted to devise a way to talk about punctuation that would communicate directly to my students, and it occurred to me to use the image of punctuation as traffic signal. Punctuation marks are simply a courtesy to the reader; they give an indication of how to proceed through the text. Because students often have reservations about this explanation, I show them examples of texts from the 1400s in which there are no punctuation marks, let alone spacing between words and sentences. What the printing press did to spacing and punctuation marks, the automobile has done to traffic signals, and we begin to look at punctuation in a new light.

Let's say, I begin, that you want to come to a full halt at the end of your line. You need a strong mark of punctuation to signal your reader to come to a complete, controlled stop. The strongest mark of punctuation we have to signal this action is the period, just as the most emphatic signal for a driver to stop is the red light. Easy enough. But what happens if you want your readers to stop for only a brief moment before proceeding? A semicolon—punctuation's equivalent to the stop sign—might be just the mark of punctuation you need. After all, the semicolon alerts the reader that two (or more) ideas are related. In much the same way, the stop sign asks the driver to pause momentarily before continuing.

Pursuing the analogy, I make a case for a yellow light or a yield sign as the equivalent of a comma. Such traffic signals provide the driver with a moment of pause (but not a stop) to take note of the surroundings before proceeding. If anything, the comma is something of an ordering device in writing; it can pull together the parts of a sentence to achieve a better sense of the whole.

At this point in my presentation, it is not uncommon for students to match the remaining marks of punctuation with other traffic signals. One student insisted that the colon was like a school-crossing sign because he envisioned a procession of children when he saw that sign. Similarly, he saw a line of entries or an explanation following the colon. Not bad for a student who had previously used punctuation marks haphazardly in his writing.

As farfetched as this comparison seems, I think it is valuable for several reasons. It speaks to students in a language they know and understand. It makes punctuation less confusing because it distinguishes among marks they once considered trivial and interchangeable. Finally, this metaphor encourages students to take their time in considering how best to direct their readers through their writing so that ideas move along effectively.

Janet Samuelson, Ohio State University, Marion Campus, Ohio

Collaborative Readers

I do not for various reasons follow a "pure" collaborative model, but I do ask students to work together on Collaborative Days set up before each written-at-home paper is due. Students bring their final drafts, clearly written, with any notes or bibliography required by the assignment. They spend the period working on their papers with a partner, each one helping the other as fully as possible.

Partners proofread for each other, of course, but only the writer of the essay may make changes, and the collaborator must be able to explain why a change is needed (students bring their handbooks to these sessions). Students read for whatever we have been working on as a class—coherence, paragraph unity, transitions, and especially liveliness. Sometimes I list on the board questions they are to answer about each other's papers. Students are also encouraged to comment on content. More important, they work on each other's thesis: Is one present? Is it properly placed? Is it appropriate to the assignment?

Often one pair exchanges papers with another; or if there's a question about, say, comma usage, they may seek out the class punctuation expert. When there are problems partners can't solve, I act as consultant, but I make sure they have first tried to resolve the issue themselves. If I am needed, I work with the pair, not with the individual writer. And I refuse to read a paper during these sessions; partners must *talk* to me about the problem.

There are many advantages in collaboration. It is easier, of course, for students to see strengths and weaknesses in someone else's work. Then, too, collaborative reading encourages students to focus on the *process* of writing: just because something has been written down doesn't mean that the paper is finished. The idea of making—and remaking—rhetorical choices comes through clearly. And finally, in reading each other's papers, students learn how someone else handled the same assignment. They are, therefore, better able to judge their own work.

Linda A. Carroll, Nassau Community College, Garden City, New York

4 Fun and Functional: Projects, Strategies, and Diversions

How to run a four-week reading marathon, how to establish an English Honorary that "does things," and how to deal with Fridays in a low-skills English class are among the projects described in this chapter. The Spelling Support System is so simple you'll marvel that you didn't think of it years ago. The Quest for the Black Crystal and the Great All-American T-Shirt Slogan Contest are two momentary diversions that you'll return to semester after semester.

Bookathon

I've used this idea with eighth-graders, and it works especially well with students who tend to read only one type of book—romances, science fiction, animal stories. Each student chooses the "very best book I've ever read" (minimum 100 pages) and registers it on a chart so duplicates are avoided. Now the job is to sell this book to classmates.

In a few days students bring their books to class prepared to act as salespersons or promoters for their books. They can make a poster, design a bookmark, dramatize a scene, read a section that leaves their classmates "dying to read more"—any tactic to convince their audience to read the book.

Students then exchange books and begin reading. When a student finishes a book, we discuss it together. I also keep a chart that shows how many times a given book has been read as well as how many books each student has read. Gift certificates from a local bookstore are given to the student who reads the most books and to the student whose book was read most frequently. The bookathon lasts about four weeks, and it's proved successful in convincing students to read a wide variety of books.

Susan Egland, Moscow Junior High School, Moscow, Idaho, and Marjorie Sillers, Sea Park Elementary School, Satellite Beach, Florida

English Honorary

The English Honorary at Fort Frye High School is an organization for students and teachers who want to share experiences in the fine arts, particularly literature. Meetings are held in members' homes or at school—or sometimes at the home of a community member who wishes to encourage the lifelong interest in the fine arts that classes try to promote (but sometimes don't). Student membership is restricted in our small, rural school to twenty-one students who have completed at least four semesters of English with at least a B average. The faculty nominates and selects members each spring. Old members induct new members, and initiation includes a ritual of literary selections and music following a buffet dinner for members and their parents. The program is held as near as possible to Shakespeare's birthday in April. A local artist has designed an emblem for the group, and a national firm has cast a small gold pin and pendant.

Activities of the Honorary include at least monthly field trips to nearby college towns to attend dramatic productions or a concert series or to be the guests of community and little theater groups. (Our group has a standing invitation to be the dress rehearsal audience for the nearby community theater.) One year we launched a full-scale production of *Androcles and the Lion*, with every member of the Honorary on stage or participating in some other way. Members may bring guests, and recently fifty-five students attended an Ohio University production of *A Mid-summer Night's Dream*. When our usual bus service was canceled, parents and school patrons volunteered to drive.

To avoid leadership by an all-too-familiar few, meeting and activity leaders shift every month. Each teacher in the English department serves as sponsor for one month's activities, and the entire department helps with the annual banquet and initiation. Department members sign up in September for the month of their choice and plan events with a student committee. Some programs our students have enjoyed include a February party where everyone dressed and acted the role of a favorite literary character, a slide show and discussion of the Hiroshima bombing, a visit from a young poet-in-residence at Hiram College, a folk night with members costumed as American folk heroes and bringing well-researched tales to tell, a poetry night with students reading their own verse or their favorites.

There are no dues, no rules, and no regularly scheduled meetings. "It's the only club I ever belonged to that *did* anything," one senior remarked.

June Berkley, Ohio University, Athens, Ohio

Read It Again, Sam

I began five years ago reading aloud to my high school students. I've had ninth through twelfth graders—General English, Beginning Reading, and College Prep—and have read to all of them.

I read primarily because I want students to get excited about a book, and I want them to share this reading experience. I read well and that gives kids who don't read well a chance to enjoy smooth reading. It also gives me a chance to spread the word about favorite books. Sometimes, I read to entertain and we merely chat about the book later. Other times I give short comprehension quizzes, both objective and essay. Some students need this point-getter. Once in a while a few questions about the book appear on a quarter or semester final.

Here are some of the books with which I've had success:

> *When the Legends Die* by Hal Borland (six times)
> *The Chocolate War* by Robert Cormier (three times)
> *I Am the Cheese* by Robert Cormier (once)
> *The Man without a Face* by Isabelle Holland (three times)
> *Listen to the Silence* by David W. Elliott (once)
> *Ordinary People* by Judith Guest (two times before the movie came out)
> *Swimmer in the Secret Sea* by William Kotzwinkle (fifteen or twenty times; it takes only 70 to 100 minutes—don't miss it!)

I'm currently reading Robert Pirsig's *Zen and the Art of Motorcycle Maintenance*. I've started reading it three or four times but have finished it only twice. Students love it or hate it. I also read short stories by Creeley, Hemingway, and LeGuin and selections from many books.

Whether the kids end up at the local community college, working at the local bank, studying at Oregon State or Stanford, fishing or logging, they have gotten back to me that they liked and remember the oral reading and sometimes that they got turned on by books in my class. I couldn't be happier.

John Foges, R. A. Long High School, Longview, Washington

Fifty-Point Friday

Fifty-Point Friday was designed for a low-skills English class (grades 9–12) in an attempt to keep poorly motivated students working on Friday afternoons, but it can be adapted for other students at other levels. At the beginning of the hour, students receive a list of activities, each with an assigned point value. The activities include worksheets and puzzles from *Scholastic Scope* and *Read* magazines, spelling and vocabulary drills, grammar and punctuation review sheets, word games, and creative writing ideas. During the hour students may choose to complete any of these activities, with their goal being to accumulate at least 50 points. When they reach 50 points, several options are available to them—completing assignments missed or not finished during the week, working on homework from another class, library reading, or playing games like Scrabble, Yahtzee, Ad-lib, and Boggle. The last choice given to them is to earn extra-credit points by continuing to do activities from Fifty-Point Friday.

The result was unplanned. Every student continued working right up to the last bell in an effort to accumulate the maximum number of points, usually between 75–85. No one wanted "free" time after 50 points had been reached. Friday afternoons are now a busy time in my classroom right up to the final bell. The free-time options remain but are never used.

Diane Franchini, Enumclaw High School, Enumclaw, Washington

Ticktacktoe Review

This activity provides a brisk review of literature, grammar, spelling, or punctuation—or combinations of these and other categories.

Draw a ticktacktoe grid on the chalkboard. Insert category labels that identify the material that has been studied and is to be reviewed. For each category on the grid you will need a list of ten or more questions.

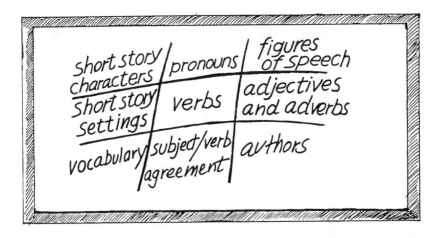

Divide the class into two teams and choose a symbol for each, traditionally O and X. Each team sends forward its first representative, and the toss of a coin determines which team begins. The first competitor selects a category, and you choose a question from the prepared list. The student has thirty seconds to respond. If the answer is correct, place the team's mark in the category square. If the answer is incorrect, the second competitor may attempt to answer the question or choose another category. The initial contestants are then replaced by the second member from each team. Questions alternate back and forth until one team scores—vertically, horizontally, or diagonally. Keep score for a given number of games and declare the higher scoring team the winner.

Martha Adams, Westlake High School, Austin, Texas

Spelling Support System

Each week write the spelling words for that particular week on file cards, one word to a card. If there are thirty students in the class, prepare thirty cards so that each student receives one. Distribute the cards with the following instructions: "In a week you will be given a spelling test on these words. You will be graded on how many of your classmates' words you spell correctly *and* on how many students in the class spell your word correctly."

Even if Lazy Larry chooses not to expend the effort to go around and learn what is on the cards of his classmates, he will still find himself besieged by classmates wanting to find out what is on *his* card and making sure that Larry learns how to spell *their* words. It's a delight to see the kids hounding each other—and over spelling!

Jeff Golub, Shelton High School, Shelton, Washington

Once upon a Time

Oral interpretation of children's literature encourages high school students to practice appropriate pitch, volume, enunciation, inflection, and rate. It's an ideal speech activity for the English classroom.

Students begin by listening to recordings of children's literature that I have checked out of the public library. Tammy Grimes's interpretation of *Where the Wild Things Are* and Ruby Dee's reading of *Why Mosquitoes Buzz in People's Ears* (both on Caedmon) are especially delightful and instructive. I distribute texts of these recordings and require students to use symbols (‖ to indicate a pause, underlining for emphasis, < for increasing volume, and so on) to chart what they hear the readers doing with their voices.

Our next step is to visit a nearby elementary school, where we are guests at a story hour in a kindergarten classroom. Before leaving, we stop at the school library to select books for our project.

Back in our own classroom, students copy their texts and mark them with the appropriate symbols. We practice reading with one another before visiting kindergartens in groups of three. Each student also prepares a short, informal talk designed to catch the interest of five-year-olds. When students perform as guest readers, the kindergarten teacher fills out a simple evaluation form.

My students enjoy this activity. They are sensitive to the response of the young audience, and this response acts as a good motivator. The activity teaches important elements of oral delivery, but it also enhances feelings of self-worth in both high school students and kindergartners.

Janice Winokur, Central High School West, Tuscaloosa, Alabama

So Happy to See All of You Here Tonight

Here's a three-minute activity that helps students develop confidence and appropriate body language before they tackle more formal speech assignments.

Most schools schedule an open house or Meet the Teacher Night, and that event is the basis for this take-off. I ask students to create an original role or to imitate a familiar teacher's mannerisms, speech patterns, and personality. In this role, they discuss course requirements, goals for the year, grading system, school regulations, and so on—just as that teacher would to a group of parents. Chuckles guaranteed.

Elena M. Loreto, Clarkstown South High School, West Nyack, New York

Skimming the Classifieds

When the *Seattle Post Intelligencer* graciously made available a large number of newspapers for use by local schools, I devised this exercise for checking skimming skills. The class enjoyed the task, and it can easily be adapted to your local paper. I present it here in abbreviated form.

Part One

Use the Want Ad Index from the *Post Intelligencer* to find the correct classified number for each item listed below. Precede each instance with "If you wanted . . ."

_____ to share an apartment   _____ to lease or rent a Porsche

_____ to rent a houseboat   _____ to share a ride

_____ to swap something   _____ to buy a cemetery plot

Part Two

Use the Classified Advertising Rates to answer the following questions.

1. What number should you call to place a want ad?
2. What does it cost per line for an ad in the daily *PI*?
3. If you run your ad for one consecutive week, how many free days can you have?

4. What is the final cancellation deadline on Saturday for Sunday's issue?

5. During what hours on weekdays may you phone in an ad?

Part Three

Use the classified ads to supply the following answers. Clue numbers from the index are given in parentheses.

1. (10) How much is the Mount Baker Park home with "sweeping view" and more?

2. (40) Where is the DK Shopping Plaza prime location, available for $10 million?

3. (80) What problem is mentioned with Triland's "must sell" acres?

4. (100) In how many different trailer parks does Brandt have mobile homes for sale?

5. (143) How much must you pay for the least expensive furnished apartment advertised?

Bruce Osborne, Rogers High School, Puyallup, Washington

Desert Dilemma

As an introduction to the novel *Deathwatch* by Robb White, I developed a discussion exercise that is similar to the Space Survival Task. In addition to leading into the novel, the exercise demonstrates one method of problem solving—listing and ranking options. The handout I use is shown below.

You are stranded in the desert dressed in summer clothing. In your desperation you have driven fifty miles off the road, and now your car is out of gas. There is nothing around you but cactus and sand, and it is 110° in the shade. You must try to reach the highway. You can carry only a limited number of things with you.

Look at the list below. Your task is to rank the fifteen items in order of their importance and utility in ensuring your survival. Place 1 by the most important item, 2 by the second most important, and so on through 15, the least important survival item. Consider what you know about the desert in making your decisions. Work individually; later we will work in groups.

_____ any part of the car
_____ sunglasses
_____ jar of Tang
_____ 4 Hershey bars
_____ map of the state
_____ box of matches
_____ silk scarf
_____ 50 feet of nylon rope
_____ first-aid kit
_____ AM-FM radio
_____ lipstick
_____ blanket
_____ slingshot
_____ pair of boots
_____ Coleman lantern

Marcie Belgard, Carmichael Junior High School, Richland, Washington

Sentence Sense

Here is an easy-to-run game that encourages students to stretch out sentence constructs and helps to pass the time on the school bus or when unavoidable delays find you with a restless group of students.

Ask a student to provide a word to begin a sentence, *jogging*, for example. (Later, students learn that *when* or *although* might be a better choice.) Each student in turn adds a word that makes sentence sense but tries to avoid giving one that completes the sentence. When students recognize the survival value of modifiers, you may need to set limitations on the number of adjectives, adverbs, and phrases that may be used.

Sue Henrich, The Langley School, McLean, Virginia

The Great American T-Shirt Slogan Contest

I sketch a T-shirt, the bigger the better, on a sheet of paper. I multicopy this sketch, something like the one below, and distribute copies to the class. Their assignment is to come up with slogans for their T-shirts that have something to do with reading. Slogans should make people want to read. Maybe they can be about a favorite book or author. Students go on to decorate their T-shirts—unusual type, logos, emblems, symbols.

I give paperbacks as prizes for the best slogans, and if students cut the T-shirts out, they make a nifty bulletin board display.

Carolyn Estes, Clinton Prairie High School, Frankfort, Indiana

The Quest for the Black Crystal

Every week I find a fellow teacher or other staff member who agrees to participate in "Riddle Master." I give that person a large black marble. Then I make up a rhymed riddle based on information about that teacher: courses taught, length of time in the school system, make or color of car, idiosyncracies of dress or speech (nothing ill-humored)—all of this is couched in mysterious, oblique language.

On Friday I read the riddle during the last three minutes of class. Students rush out to find the keeper of the black crystal. At the end of the semester the student who holds the most black marbles is named Riddle Master and receives an appropriate prize. Students may be used as the subjects of riddles instead of or in addition to faculty members.

Kathy A. Fisher, Highland High School, Medina, Ohio

From A to Z in English Class

Here's a review exercise for the odd moment. It can be assigned individually, but it's probably more fun when done as a small-group competition. Dictionaries are allowed.

Test your knowledge of terms we use in English class—from A to Z. The word to be provided in each blank begins with the letter to the left.

A _____ modify nouns and pronouns.

B _____ is a main state-of-being verb.

C _____ have subjects and predicates but are only parts of sentences.

D _____ is the kind of sentence that makes a statement.

E _____ is the punctuation mark that follows a strong interjection.

F _____ is the tense that refers to something that will be or will happen.

G _____ are verbals useds as nouns.

H _____ is the punctuation mark used to separate syllables.

I _____ is the part of speech that shows emotion.

J _____ is what conjunctions do between or among elements of a sentence.

K _____ is the past tense of the verb *to know*.

L _____ is the kind of verb that joins a subject and predicate nominative.

M _____ represent something as if it were something else: "Time is but the stream I go a-fishing in." (Thoreau)

N _____ name persons, places, things, or qualities.

O _____ receive the actions of verbs.

P _____ substitute for nouns.

Q _____ are interrogative sentences.

R _____ occur when two sentences are written together without clarifying punctuation.

S _____ have subjects, predicates, and sense.

T _____ indicates the time expressed by a verb.

U _____ is the opposite of hyperbole.

V _____ show action or state of being.

W _____ is the possessive form of *who*.

X _____ is a combining form meaning strange or foreign. Three words built with that form are _____, _____, and _____.

Y _____ is the word usually understood in an imperative sentence.

Z _____ is the eagerness you have shown in completing this Z_____ exercise.

Here are the answers, but rather than reading them aloud, have the class work out an answer key on which everyone agrees. Write it on the board so that students may check their answers on this not-for-grades review.

adjectives	join	sentences
be	knew	tense
clauses	linking	understatement
declarative	metaphors	verbs
exclamation point	nouns	whose
future	objects	xen-, xeno-
gerunds	pronouns	you
hyphen	questions	zest, zany
interjection	run-ons	

Alicia J. Olive, Rabaut Junior High School, Washington, DC